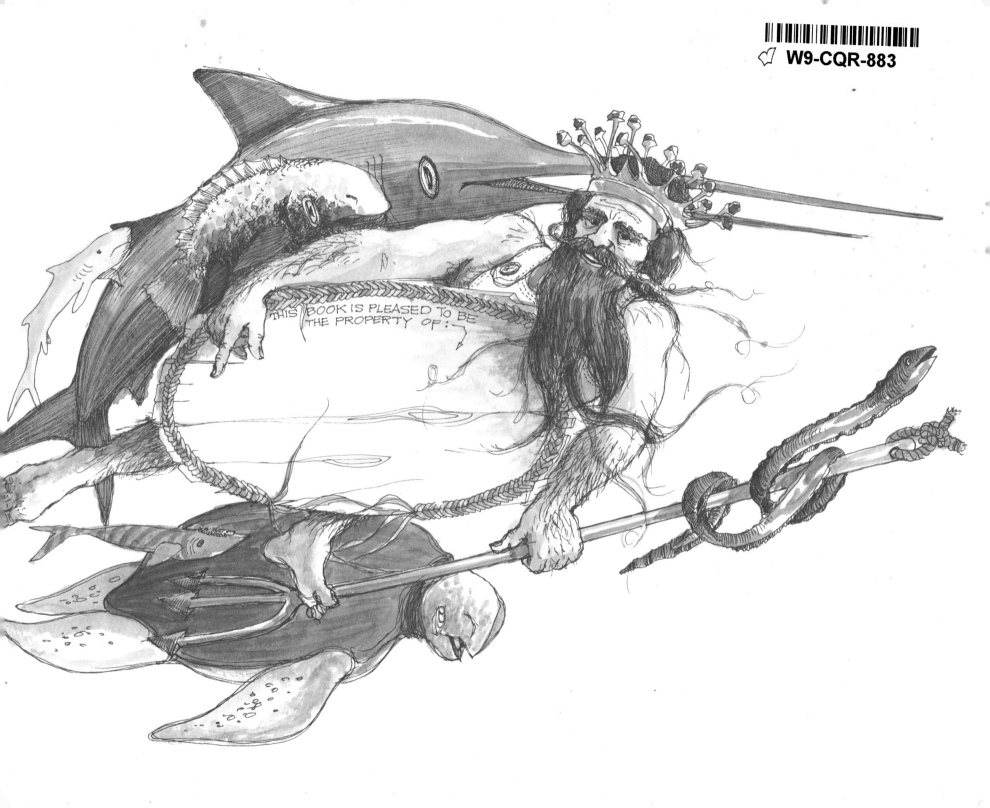

W9-CQR-883

THIS BOOK IS PLEASED TO BE
THE PROPERTY OF:

the Art and Industry *of* SANDCASTLES

being: an illustrated guide to basic constructions along with

divers information devised by one Jan Adkins, a wily fellow.

All rights reserved. no part of this book may be reproduced or transmitted in any form or by any means, electronic or mechanical, including recording, photocopying, or by any information storage and retrieval system, without permission in writing from the publisher, so watch yourself.

first published in the united states of america in 1971 by the beneficence of walker publishing company, incorporated.

paperback edition published in 1994 by walker publishing company, inc.

published simultaneously in canada by thomas allen and son, markham, ontario

LIBRARY of CONGRESS CATALOGUE CARD NUMBER
76-141615
ISBN: 0-8027-0336-4
ISBN: 0-8027-7205-6 (paper)

printed in the united states of america by a magic process of jake's.

copyright ©1971 by that rascal, Jan Adkins

THIS ODD BOOK IS FONDLY DEDICATED TO MY VERY GOOD FRIENDS WHO ARE NOT OLD ENOUGH TO LOSE MAGIC—WITH LUCK THEY CAN KEEP IT A LONG TIME. ONLY A FEW OF THEM ARE HERE, HELLO TO THE OTHERS

Miss Annabanana

Erin of Warr Street

Sir Robert of Wareham

Sir John of Columbus

Stevie the Beetle

Stevie the Wizard

Jennifer the Obscure

Peter the Driver

and Tum

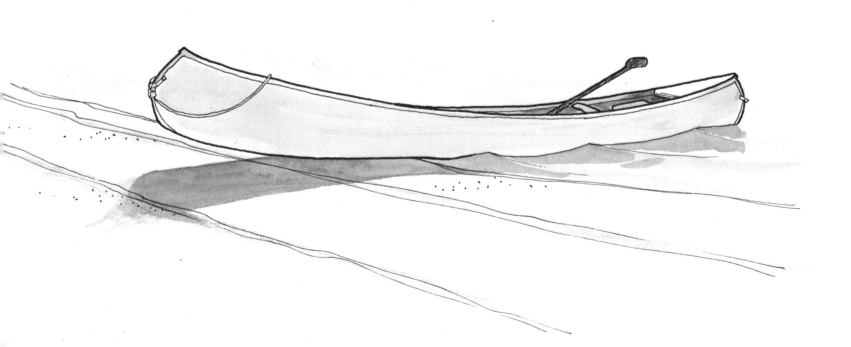

What is a sandcastle? It is your private legend, a fortress made of sand and imagination for your own heroes, a stronghold for your daydreams. It is the strong desire to build, to create forms with your own meanings. It is most of all your own, out of your head, made by your hands.

I

Sandcastles are not just fooged down on the sand, what did you think? A castle must be impressively strong and exceedingly clever to protect its knights and ladies. You will have to learn something about baileys, parapets, crenelations and keeps — you will have to build as men built for the kings of the green kingdoms of chivalry.

The building of a castle needed:

GENERATIONS OF WORKERS; HUGE WHEEL-WINCHES, RIGGERS, DRAY-CARTS, CART-DRIVERS, OXEN....

AND MINSTRELS IN GOOD VOICE TO KEEP THINGS GOING ♪ ....

HOD-CARRIERS, MASONS, TRENCHERS, CARPENTERS, BLACKSMITHS, WATER-BOYS, AND THE MASTERBUILDER....

If you take several generations to build a castle, you will not get back for supper on time. If you get all those masons and trenchers, and all the other workmen together on the beach, it would be a better idea to have a clambake than to build a castle. You will not need carts and oxen, nor a great wheel-winch, but there are a few things you could use:

YOU WILL NEED A PILE OF SAND...
(YOU COULD USE A BEACH FOR THAT),
A SMALL SHOVEL WOULD BE HANDY, A TROWEL OR WIDE PUTTY KNIFE OR SPATULA, SOME FORMS FOR

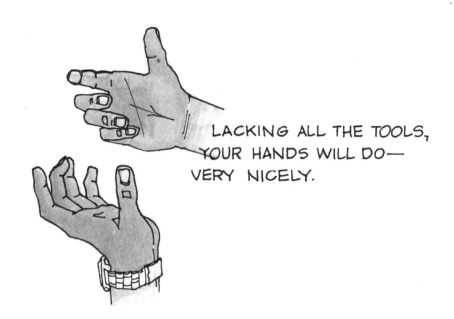

LACKING ALL THE TOOLS,
YOUR HANDS WILL DO—
VERY NICELY.

YOU'LL NEED A MASTER-BUILDER (THAT'S YOU)....

MOULDING, A MINSTREL IF HANDY (YOU MIGHT SING YOUR OWN SONGS)...

IV

Saxon forts were not what we think of as castles; they were only wooden stockade walls on a mound built up from the earth taken out of the moat, a narrow bridge approached the single gate. The chief and his soldiers lived within it, protected by the moat, mound, walls, and their own arrows and swords. The times were violent, the warlord had to protect his men his treasure, and his life.

build up the shape with your hands— start with a mound from the shovel

cut the damp sand cleanly with a trowel or spatula

smooth up a frosting of very wet sand

load buckets even with their tops—
overload smaller
forms, scraping the
tops even.

turn it over with
a THUMP!

RAP! the bottom
and edges

lift off the form
and smooth the tower.

One of the first kinds of castles in old England was the Norman keep. It was a simple tower with its one entrance high above the ground. On the ground floor were storerooms for food and wine and treasure with trapdoors to the main hall above. The entrance led into the main hall—everyone ate together there, they listened to lute players or minstrels who sat in the loft above. Built into the thick walls (12 to 16 feet) on this floor was the Pit, a tiny bottle-shaped room for prisoners entered from above by a trap door (it was no fun in the Pit). The guards and servants slept in the main hall, but the Chief had his rooms on the third floor, below the roof where archers and stone throwers protected the keep from behind a parapet.

PARAPET

CHIEF'S ROOMS

LOFT

STAIRS

THE MAIN HALL

ENTRANCE

VAULTS

PIT

a norman keep in 1100

You could find a gloomy crag in the rocks and build up a thick, round tower as forbidding as possible: the Black Tower of Roumeli Hissar. It was 120 feet high, its walls were 24 thick; feeble light seeped into the stairways, no light at all reached the dark inner rooms where prisoners, jars of oil and boxes of treasure or spices were kept and forgotten. In the darkness at the end of a dark stairs was a sudden drop into a deep pit — it was called an "oubliette", and unwanted people were sent up the wrong stairs to fetch something.... did they ever come back down? Wicked keeps like the Black Tower make people think all castles are sad.

"OUBLIETTE"

Black Tower of
Roumeli Hissar

VIII

MOUND UP SAND BETWEEN
MOLDED TOWERS AND
SHAPE WITH YOUR HANDS

CUT OUT THE FOR
OF THE WALL FRO
THE PACKED MOU

Walls are the curtain of safety around your stronghold.

CUT DOWN, ACROSS, AND
LIFT OUT THE PARAPET
WALK FOR YOUR GUARDS

IX

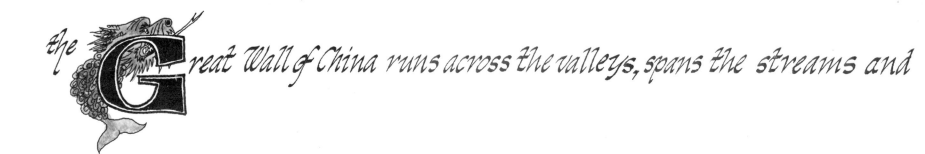

the **G**reat Wall of China runs across the valleys, spans the streams and

coils over the mountains of more than 1500 miles of northern China.

It was high enough to keep out Mongol invaders, and broad enough for a chariot. It was built around 210 b.c. by order of the Emperor of Ch'in, from whom China took its name.

Hadrian's Wall was built around 100 a.d., spanning the width of Britain, 73 miles, connecting forts placed at intervals to resist invading Picts and Scots from the North.

When you build your wall against the sea, you will lose, but losing to the sea is the natural way of things by the sea.

HADRIAN'S WALL   GREAT WALL OF CHINA

THE HILL OR MOAT AROUND
A CASTLE PREVENTED RUDE
PEOPLE FROM WHEELING A
HIGH SCALING TOWER (CALLED
A "CAT") UP TO THE WALLS, TOO
HIGH FOR MEN WITH SHAKY LAD-
DERS. THE THICK WALLS SHRUGGED
OFF HEAVY STONES THROWN BY MACHINES
LIKE THIS ONAGER (OR CATAPULT). MEN DEFENDING THE
WALLS DUCKED FROM
ARROWS AND SPEARS
BEHIND OPENINGS
IN THE PARAPET
CALLED
"CRENELATIONS".

What did a castle defend against?

IT DEFENDED THE PEACE INSIDE ITS WALLS; IT DEFENDED AN ARMY SMALLER THAN THE ARMY OUTSIDE; OR IT COULD DEFEND A KING; AS MANY CASTLES IMPRISONED KINGS AND QUEENS OR OTHER IMPORTANT PEOPLE; A CASTLE KEPT FOOD AND DRINK TO LAST THROUGH LONG SIEGES; BUT IT KEPT PEACE MOST CAREFULLY.

What did a castle defend?

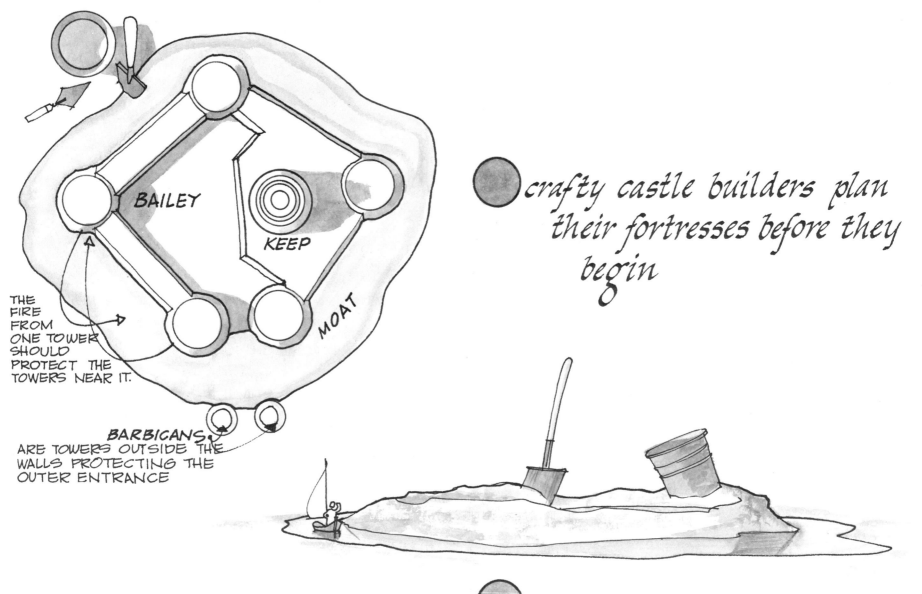

BAILEY

KEEP

MOAT

THE FIRE FROM ONE TOWER SHOULD PROTECT THE TOWERS NEAR IT.

BARBICANS. ARE TOWERS OUTSIDE THE WALLS PROTECTING THE OUTER ENTRANCE

● crafty castle builders plan their fortresses before they begin

● dig the moat and pile a rough wall inside it with the sand...

mold towers from the
moat-sand,

mold walls between towers,

now build up the
keep within...

You must not think that a castle was a dark or dreary place to live; the gentlemen and gentlewomen who made a castle their home thought it was a wonderful, warm place. In the Summer the thick stone walls kept a castle cool and dim; there were high walls and watchtowers from which to catch a breeze; fountains and deep cisterns in the cobbled courtyard made that a pleasant place to play games with a feather-filled ball or teach a crow to talk. In the Winter the great hall was bright and warm with oil lamps, torches, and fires built on raised stones — smoke escaped through holes in the roof and birds roosted on the high beams in the warm smoke; the castle smelled of sweet applewood and rich pine smoke. You might like a castle-home.

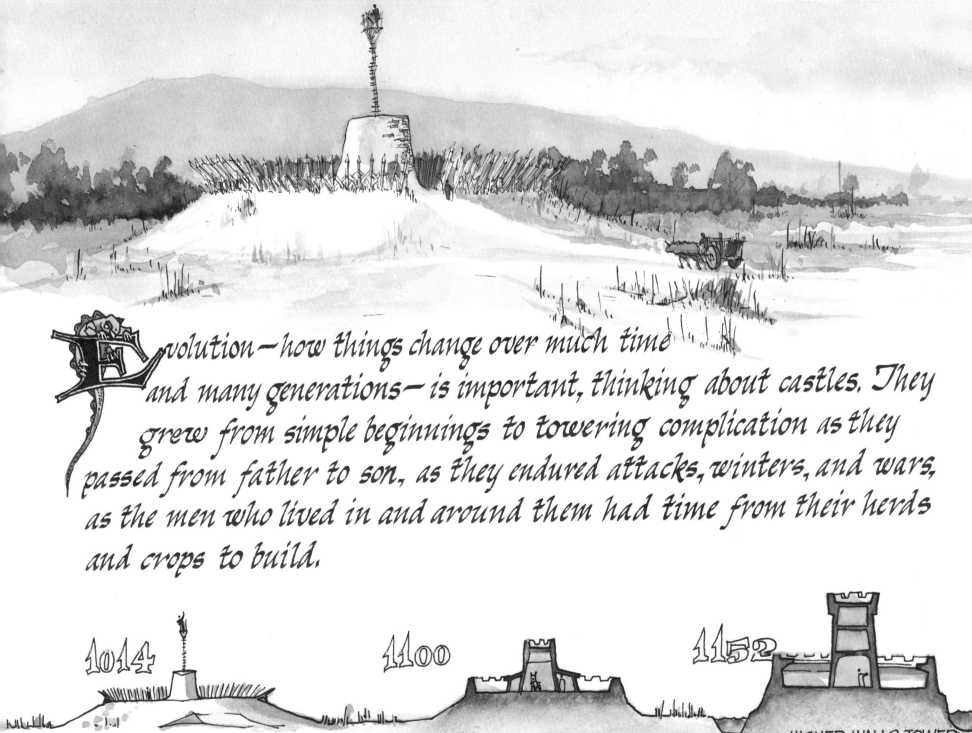

volution—how things change over much time and many generations—is important, thinking about castles. They grew from simple beginnings to towering complication as they passed from father to son, as they endured attacks, winters, and wars, as the men who lived in and around them had time from their herds and crops to build.

1014
THE FORT BEGINS WITH A STONE TOWER, LOG-STAKE WALLS...

1100
THE TOWER GROWS AND THE WALLS ARE REPLACED WITH STONE...

1152
HIGHER WALLS, TOWER; A MOAT IS ADDED....

301

THE ORIGINAL TOWER IS A
LOOKOUT, CORNER TOWERS PROTECT WALLS...

1628

EVOLUTION REVERSES, THE LORD MOVES TO A
TOWNHOUSE IN TIMES OF PEACE, THE CASTLE DECAYS.

XIV

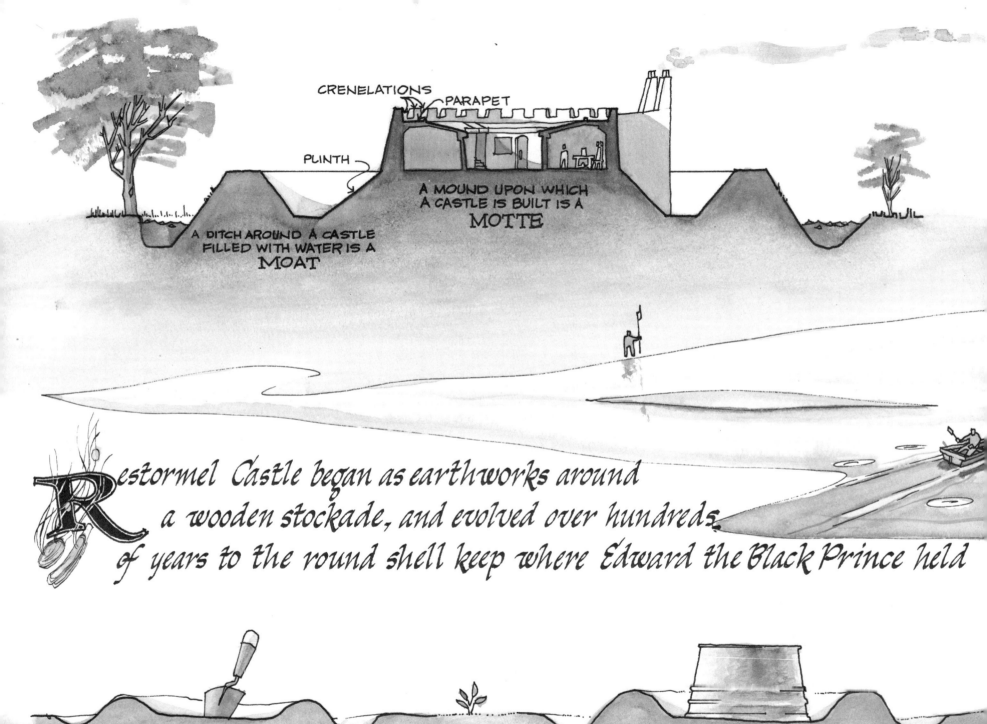

CRENELATIONS

PARAPET

PLINTH

A DITCH AROUND A CASTLE
FILLED WITH WATER IS A
MOAT

A MOUND UPON WHICH
A CASTLE IS BUILT IS A
MOTTE

Restormel Castle began as earthworks around a wooden stockade, and evolved over hundreds of years to the round shell keep where Edward the Black Prince held

SAND FROM THE MOAT BEGINS THE EARTHWORK WALLS...

A LARGE BUCKET IS A GOOD MOLD TO START
THE MOTTE AND KEEP

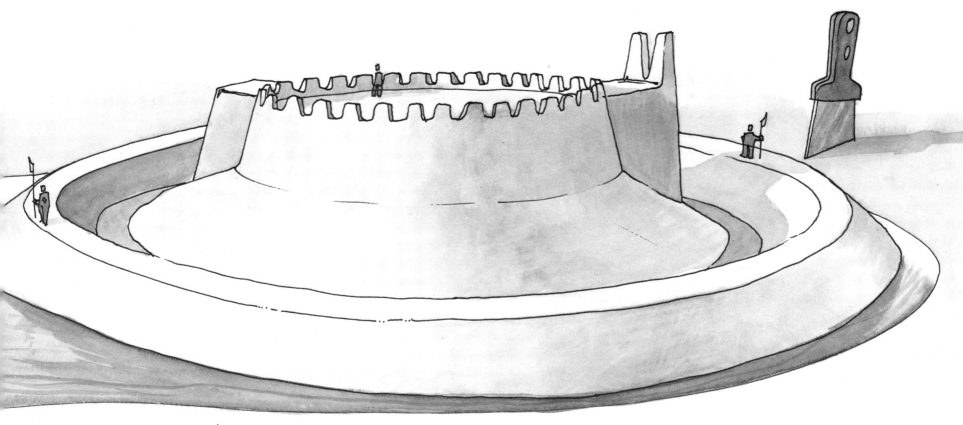

...ourt in 1360. *Sand castles evolve, too, over a shorter period so that you can hold court before the tide comes in.*

ADD A PLINTH (A SLANTED BASE) TO THE KEEP...   FORM THE CRENELATIONS ON THE PARAPET AND
ADD THE CHAPEL .... HOLD COURT.   XV

~1250 A ROUND KEEP FOR A WARLORD; BUILT, PERHAPS, ON THE ANCIENT SITE OF MANY REFUGES.

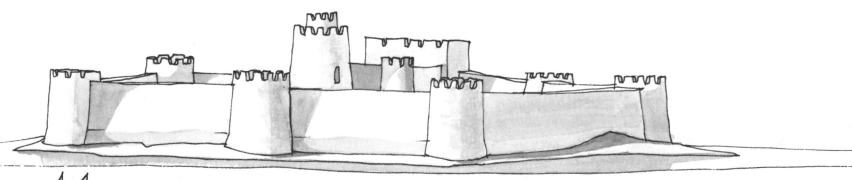

~1400 A WALL IS BUILT AROUND A PARCEL OF LAND TO KEEP PART OF THE VILLAGE AND ALL THE VILLAGERS INSIDE DURING ATTACKS.

Pembroke Castle evolved, as your castle might. At first it was a families of the village had time to work at it, and as times made

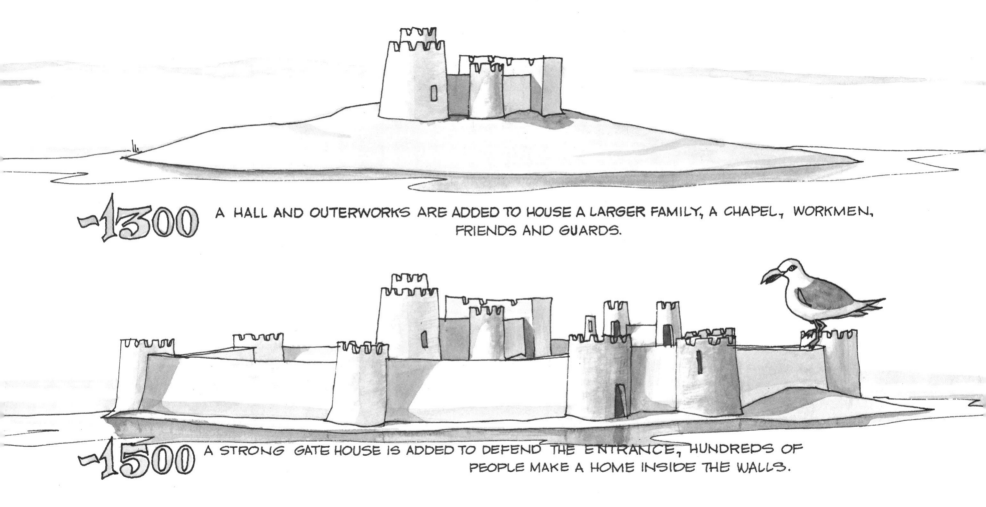

-1300 A HALL AND OUTERWORKS ARE ADDED TO HOUSE A LARGER FAMILY, A CHAPEL, WORKMEN, FRIENDS AND GUARDS.

-1500 A STRONG GATE HOUSE IS ADDED TO DEFEND THE ENTRANCE, HUNDREDS OF PEOPLE MAKE A HOME INSIDE THE WALLS.

simple tower keep, and it grew as the Earls of Pembroke and the
it necessary to have a greater, stronger refuge.

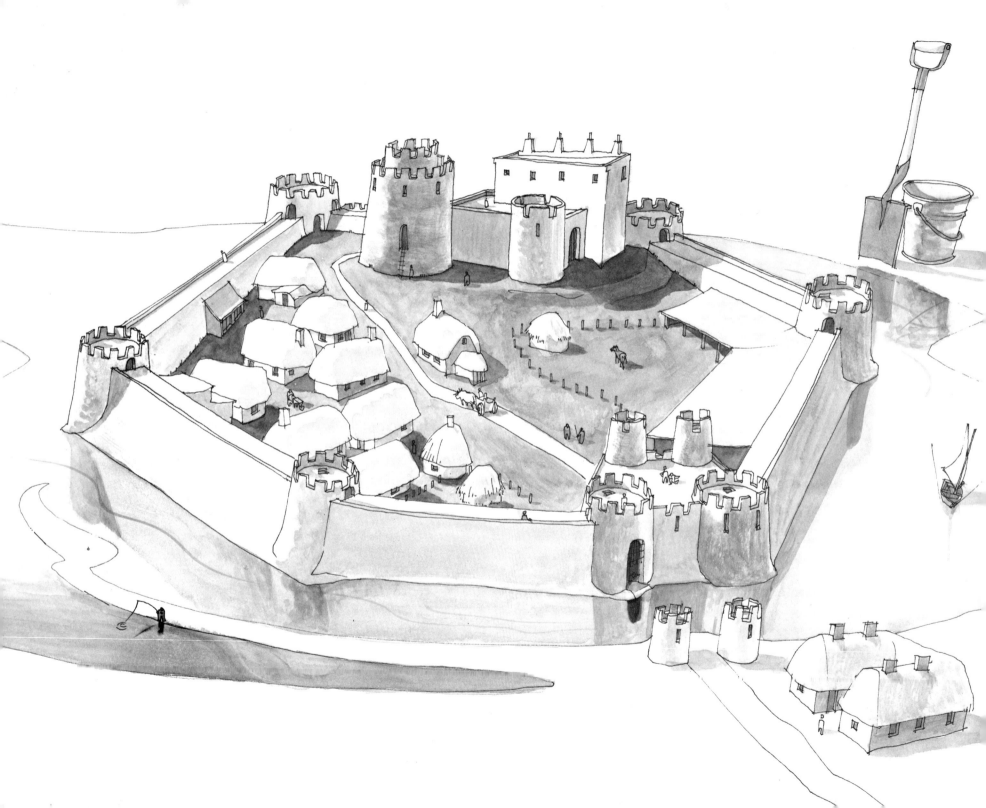

As a castle grew, a village grew around it. People built their cottages near the castle to be near its protection. In times of trouble the villagers rushed to be protected by the castle and to help defend it. Tradesmen set up their workshops in castle-villages to deal with people travelling to the castle, for it was the center of life in those times! It was marketplace, meeting hall, a barn for the countryside's crops, a courthouse, the chapel was within its walls, fairs and entertainments were given in its courtyard......
Where a castle was raised, a town began.

Night life at the castle was not dreary, it was full of talk and music. In the cool evening the ladies and gentlemen ate together. The evening meal was the social time of the day, when guests brought news from far places, plans were discussed and storytellers called bards sang old tales of heroes. Later, the ladies sewed, sang together, and stitched stories from history into colorful tapestries to hang over the glassless windows.

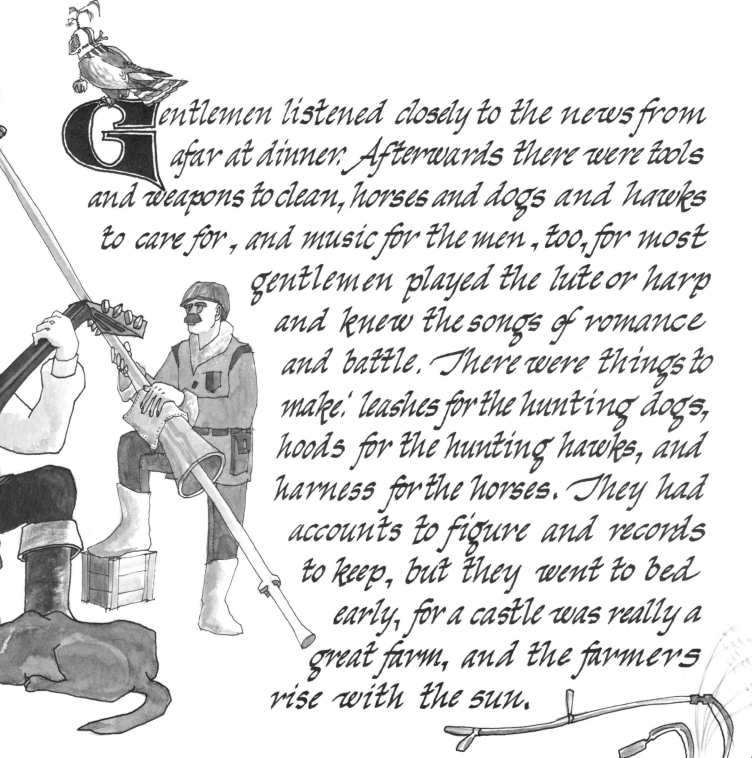

Gentlemen listened closely to the news from afar at dinner. Afterwards there were tools and weapons to clean, horses and dogs and hawks to care for, and music for the men, too, for most gentlemen played the lute or harp and knew the songs of romance and battle. There were things to make: leashes for the hunting dogs, hoods for the hunting hawks, and harness for the horses. They had accounts to figure and records to keep, but they went to bed early, for a castle was really a great farm, and the farmers rise with the sun.

Concentric defences are widening rings of walls and towers placed in a way that allows the defenders to retreat behind a second wall if attackers manage to overrun the first. The courtyards between the walls are called baileys. The last line of defence was usually the keep.

1st LINE of DEFENSE   2nd LINE   3rd LINE   FINAL LINE/THE KEEP

KEEP   KEEP   KEEP   KEEP

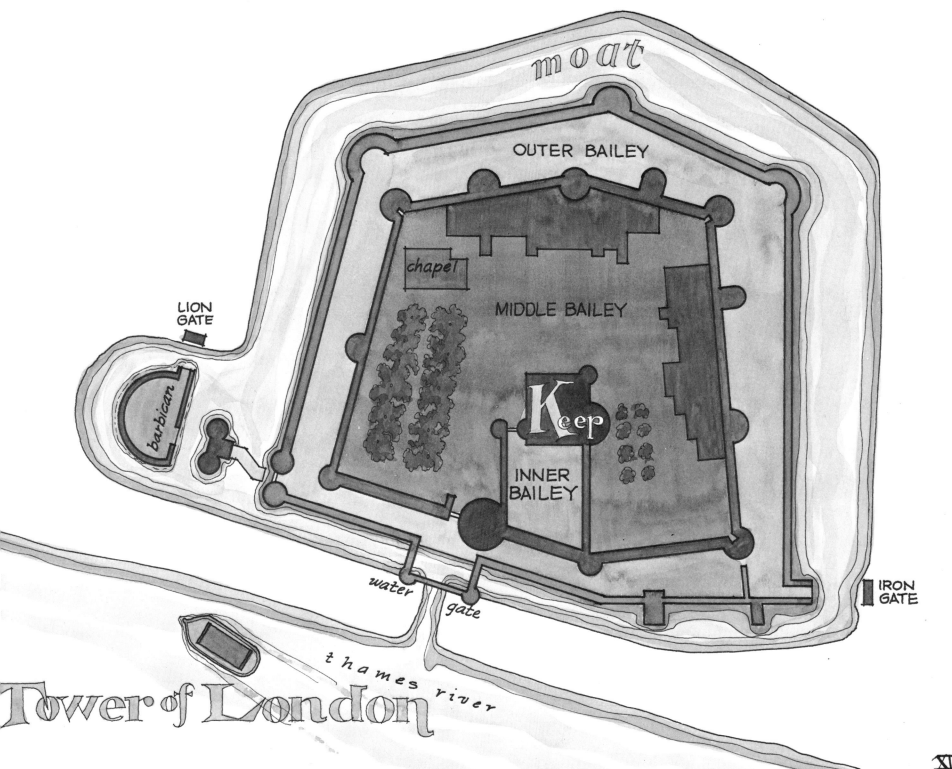

moat

OUTER BAILEY

chapel

MIDDLE BAILEY

LION
GATE

barbican

Keep

INNER
BAILEY

IRON
GATE

water

gate

thames river

Tower of London

XIX

The Tower of London stands by the river Thames in London today, an example of concentric defence and a somber reminder of the noble and royal heads that kept their appointments with the headsman's axe here. You must build a castle with the tide; using the materials of the sea, you will be obliged to accept the fortunes of the sea. A castle is yours, yes, but only until the sea takes it. Build far enough from the incoming tide to finish, but near enough to allow the waves to claim their rightful property. To give the sea its due is part of the rules.

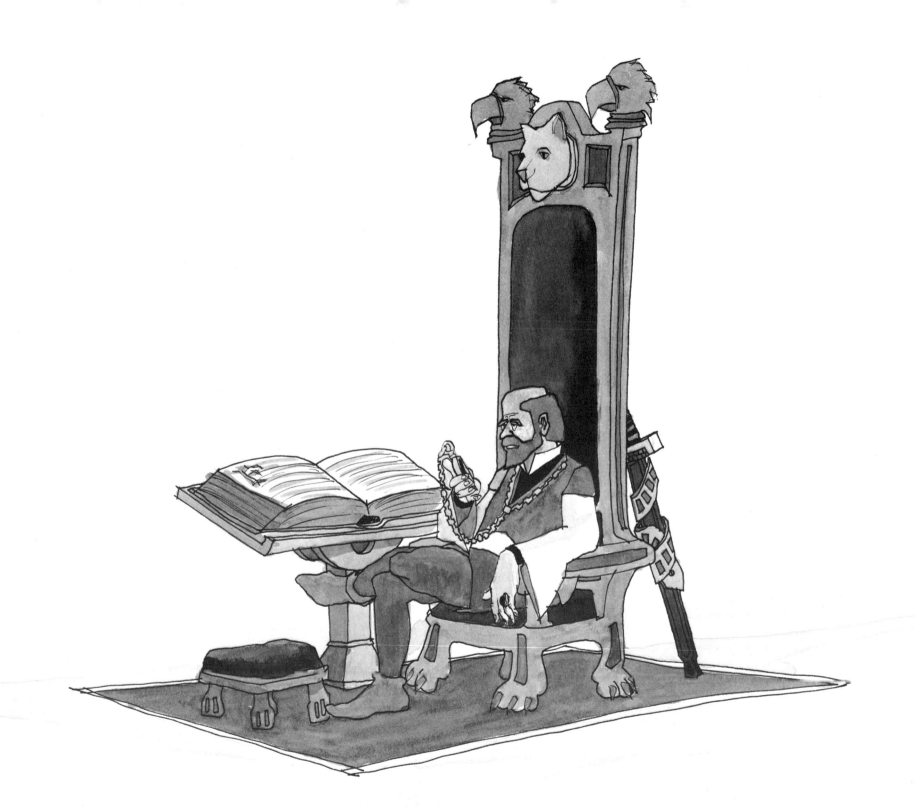

The Lord of the hall was the master of the land—builder, farmer, hunter, soldier, scholar, mayor—he was leader, planner, defender, enforcer, jury and judge. He decided what crops to plant and helped to plant them; the laws were his to make and uphold; every person within the boundaries of his land was his subject and owed him service as a soldier, time for gathering crops and labor in building defences. The lord owed his subjects leadership, a fatherly justice, careful planning, wisdom.
In turn, the lord owed his king service, labor, and allegiance.

Masterbuilders chose places hard to attack, easy to defend.
You may build anywhere to defend your castle:

ON AN ISLAND OF SAND OR AN ISLAND OF ROCK; YOU MAY BUILD BETWEEN ROCKS....

BY A FOREST OF SEA GRASSES

ON THE ROCKY RIDGEBACK OF A JETTY

ON AN ISTHMUS (A NECK OF LAND CONNECTED BY A NARROW STRIP TO THE MAINLAND)

XXII

Crenelations, behind which defenders duck to avoid arrows.

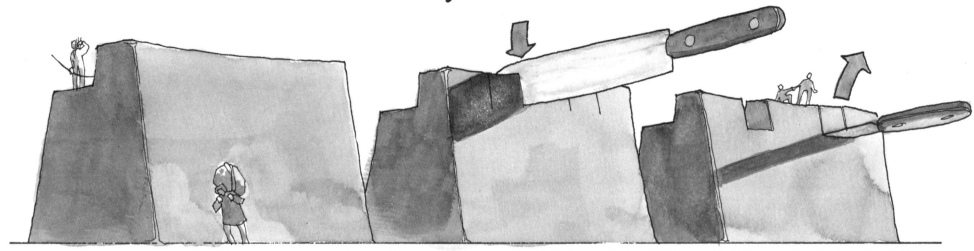

CUT OUT THE PARAPET WALK, MAKE CUTS DOWN TO WALK DEPTH THE WIDTH OF THE SPATULA APART, LIFT UP AND OUT.

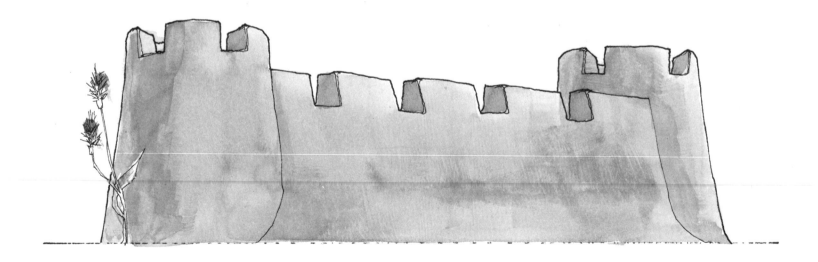

Entryways, so as to get in and out.

WHILE SAND IS STILL DAMP, TUNNEL INTO ONE SIDE WITH A SPOON, THEN THE OTHER SIDE, KEEPING THE PASSAGE ROUNDED.

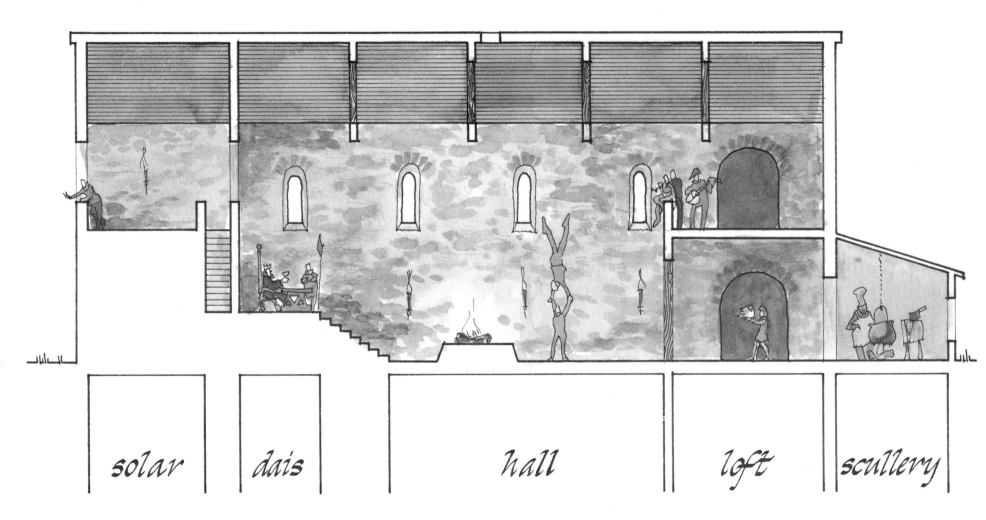

solar   dais   hall   loft   scullery

The **G**reat hall was the center of the castle's life. Here the lord sat in the place of honor on his raised Dais and held court or ate the huge feasts prepared by his cooks in the Scullery. While the king, his guests, and the rest of the castle folk ate, they watched jongleurs or acrobats and listened to musicians playing in the Musician's Loft. After his meal the lord retired to his Solar above.

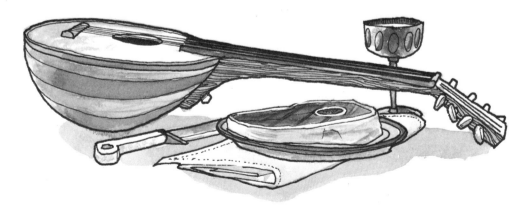

GreatHall

IN A SMOKEY SHED
STACKED WITH
CHARCOAL AND BARS
OF IRON YOU WOULD
FIND THE
blacksmith
MAKING ARMOUR,
KITCHEN KNIVES, AND
EVERY BIT OF USEFUL
METAL IN THE CASTLE.

THE *ostler*
WOULD BE RUSTLING
AROUND THE STABLE,
CURRYING HORSES,
FEEDING THEM, CARING
FOR SADDLES, HARNESS,
AND CARTS.

Castle folk— there were special people in a castle you might like to meet.

THE *master-at-arms* WAS PROBABLY AN OLDER KNIGHT UNABLE TO RIDE OUT ON DIFFICULT MISSIONS; YOU WOULD FIND HIM IN THE COURTYARD INSTRUCTING YOUNG SQUIRES IN THE SKILLS OF DEFENCE AND THE SPORTS OF TOURNAMENTS.

THE *alchemist* WAS THE CASTLE'S DOCTOR, A LEARNED MAN WHO EXPLORED THE DARK SECRETS OF PHYSICS AND CHEMISTRY WITH THE CRUDE TOOLS AVAILABLE IN HIS DAY.

XXVI

IN A SUNNY GALLERY OF THE CASTLE CROWDED WITH CAGES AND CALLED THE "MEWS", YOU WOULD FIND THE *austringer,* WHO TRAINED THE HAWKS, EAGLES AND FALCONS, AND FLEW THEM TO CATCH BIRDS, RABBITS AND SQUIRRELS. THE *master of hounds* RAN THE PACK OF HUNTING DOGS THAT HELPED GATHER GAME FOR THE CASTLE TABLES. ANIMALS EARNED THEIR KEEP, THEN. HE FED AND COMBED THEM, NURSED THEM, HE SLEPT NEAR THEM, HE WAS THEIR FRIEND.

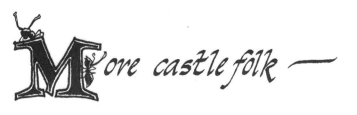

More castle folk —

NOT MANY PEOPLE COULD READ OR WRITE IN THE DAYS OF GREAT STONE WALLS. THE *scribe* (WHO WAS OFTEN A MONK) WROTE LETTERS, RECORDED CROPS AND PURCHASES, AND KEPT A DAILY JOURNAL OF THE CASTLE AND CASTLE FOLK. AS YOUNG AS EIGHT, THE *page* BEGAN HIS TRAINING AS A KNIGHT, SERVING AT TABLE TO LEARN MANNERS AND COURT GRACES.

A foolish man built his house upon the sand...

And the rain descended, and the floods came...

XXVIII

And the wind blew and beat upon that house; and it fell;

and the fall of that house was great.

Matthew 7 : 26,27

XXIX